Bookmaking Bonanza
Creative Bookmaking Ideas to Motivate Beginning Readers and Writers

D1309385

Written by
Kimberly Jordano and Kim Adsit

Editor: Kim Cernek
Illustrator: Darcy Tom
Cover Illustrator: Rick Grayson
Designer: Moonhee Pak
Cover Designer: Moonhee Pak
Art Director: Tom Cochrane
Project Director: Carolea Williams

Table of Contents

Introduction

Most every child delights in changing an everyday object into a functional tool. Whether it is a drum made from a pot and two spoons or a telephone fashioned from a banana, a child can turn just about anything into a prop for a story or an adventure. *Bookmaking Bonanza* capitalizes on children's imaginations and their talent for pretending to help them develop fundamental reading and writing skills.

This resource shows you how to help children transform empty cereal boxes, paper napkins, and other household objects into books that explore the five critical areas of balanced reading instruction: **phonemic awareness, phonics, fluency, vocabulary,** and **text comprehension.** It also explains how to expand 51 different research-based, classroom-tested bookmaking activities into modeled or shared writing lessons that teach basic skills and reinforce reading strategies.

The clever ideas in *Bookmaking Bonanza* motivate beginning readers and writers to do their best work. Children are encouraged to express their creativity as they practice beginning reading skills that include one-to-one correspondence, left-to-right orientation, top-to-bottom orientation, letter formation, picture clues, and chunking. They will also explore literacy concepts such as fiction, nonfiction, poetry, rhyme, and sentence structure, and cross-curricular skills in math and science.

Clear directions for making individual and class books come with reproducible patterns and sentence frames, which makes it easy for you to incorporate the ideas in *Bookmaking Bonanza* into your literacy program. Choose a book idea and help children make it as directed, or tailor the design to meet the needs of your curriculum. Children will become confident readers and writers as they construct and personalize their own developmentally appropriate, thematic books.

Children love stories—especially those they write themselves. *Bookmaking Bonanza* gives you the tools to expand writing time into a literacy adventure!

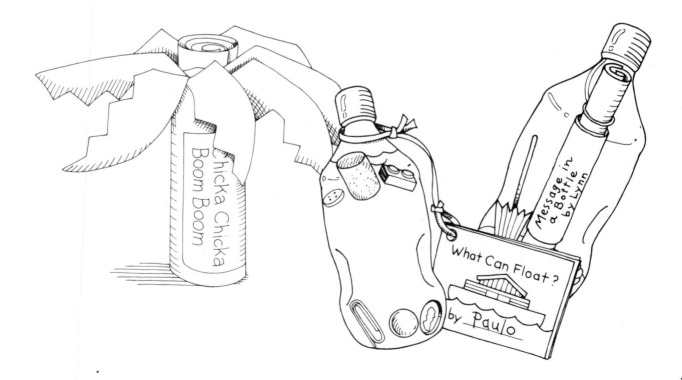

How to Use This Resource

Bookmaking Bonanza features 20 different types of books for you and your class to assemble. Straightforward directions are accompanied by clear illustrations to help you and your students construct each book with ease.

Two or more activity ideas are presented for each type of book. As you become comfortable constructing these "art project readers," you will be able to use your own creative ideas to modify these books to meet the developmental level of your class and the curricular objectives of your district.

Put Reading First

Use some of the following suggestions to help your students explore the five critical areas of balanced reading instruction (phonemic awareness, phonics, fluency, vocabulary, and text comprehension) as they write and read their books.

Phonemic awareness concentrates on the sound units (phonemes) used to form spoken words. It helps children learn to read and spell new words. Encourage children to identify and manipulate the beginning, middle, and ending sounds of words they will use in their books.

Phonics helps children associate sounds to written symbols (i.e., the alphabet). It improves word recognition, spelling, and comprehension. Say the sounds of the letters you use to write the books.

Fluency is the ability to read text with ease. A fluent reader automatically recognizes words, and thereby reads quickly, confidently, and with freedom to concentrate on comprehension. Encourage children to read and reread their books to promote fluency.

Vocabulary includes the words we use to communicate. A good reader understands the meaning of words encountered in print. Introduce children to new vocabulary when you begin a new book project, and encourage them to use these words in their writing.

Comprehension is an understanding of what is being read. An active reader uses knowledge about language, reading strategies, and the world to understand and discuss text. Ask children questions about the books they write, and encourage them to question each other about their books.

Other Ideas to Make Reading Fun

✓ Make a sample book, and read it aloud to your class.
✓ Read aloud your book again, and invite children to chorally read with you.
✓ Have children make their own books, and encourage them to read their books alone.
✓ Invite children to read their books with a partner.
✓ Send home the books for children to read to family and friends.

Materials

✓ construction paper
  (any size)
✓ white paper
✓ stapler
✓ pencils
✓ rulers
✓ scissors

Lift-the-Flap Books

Give each child a piece of construction paper. Tell children to place their paper on a flat surface and place two pieces of white paper that are the same size on top of it. Ask children to fold their papers in half and staple along the creased edge. Help children use a pencil and a ruler to draw several parallel lines at equal distances across the cover. Have them cut along the lines through the top cover and papers (leave the back cover intact) to make flaps.

A Teddy Bear's Picnic

Skills
✓ identifying beginning sounds
✓ connecting sounds and letters
✓ improving fluency
✓ writing numerals
✓ counting

Give each child a **9" x 12" (23 cm x 30.5 cm) piece of brown and white construction paper,** and use the directions on page 5 to help children make a lift-the-flap book. Show children how to cut off the corners of the book to make a basket. Give each child a **Bear reproducible (page 8)** to cut apart. Have children color their bear and glue it to the top of their book (the bound edge) so that it appears that the bear is peering over the top of a picnic basket. Give each child a **decorated paper napkin** to glue at an angle beneath the bear's chin. Invite children to paint white crisscrosses on the basket to give it a weaved texture. Help children cut a handle from another piece of brown construction paper and glue it to the top corners so that it is positioned over the bear's head. Tell children to write their name after the title and glue it on their basket. Ask them to name the beginning sounds of *Teddy* and *Bear*. Have children name the beginning letters and write *T* and *B* on the first two blank lines of each sentence strip. Invite children to write a number from one to five on the last blank line of five of the sentences. Ask them to glue one of these five sentence strips to the top of the first five flaps of their book. Tell children to glue the remaining sentence strip to the last flap. Invite children to read aloud their sentences and draw the number of pieces of fruit that are designated. For example, a child could draw five strawberries below *Teddy Bear ate 5*.

A Teddy Bear's Picnic by Jaden

Carrot Book

Give each child a **9" x 12" (23 cm x 30.5 cm) piece of orange construction paper,** and show children how to place it in a landscape orientation. Have children fold the paper in half lengthwise, and show them how to cut their paper into a carrot shape. Tell children to cut through the top orange paper to make three equal sections. Caution children that they should not cut past the creased line near the creased end to keep the book intact. Ask them to fold a piece of **green paper** in half, cut out a leafy stem, and glue the bottom part of it to one end of the carrot to make a fourth flap.

Choose four word family rimes (e.g., *-an, -it, -ot, -ig*), and write them on the board. Invite children to write a different rime on each separate top flap of their carrot. Ask them to read the rime on their first flap (e.g., *-an*) and write three to five words that feature the rime (e.g., *can, fan, man, pan, ran*) on the flap below. Encourage children to repeat the steps with the three remaining rimes. Write *I Can Read Word Families!* on the cover of each child's book, and have children write their name beside the title. Invite children to exchange and read each other's books.

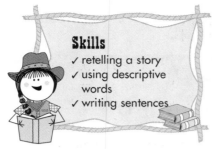
The Lady with the Alligator Purse

Give each child a **9" x 12" (23 cm x 30.5 cm) piece of light green construction paper,** and use the directions on page 5 to help children make a lift-the-flap book with four flaps. Ask children to cut two triangles from a different piece of light green paper and glue them to the top and bottom of the back of their book to make a head and tail. Tell children to glue small **wiggly eyes** or eyes cut from white paper to the top triangle. Have children cut small triangles from **white construction paper** and glue them around two sides of the same triangle to make teeth. Tell children to cut four feet from green paper and glue two to each side of the back cover.

Read aloud *The Lady with the Alligator Purse* by **Nadine Bernard Westcott (Little Brown & Company),** and have children retell the story. Encourage children to describe the physical characteristics of the lady. Cut sheets of white construction paper in half lengthwise, and give one to each child. Have children use a glue stick to attach their paper to the inside back cover of their book. Tell them to open the first flap and draw a picture of the lady's head. Ask children to draw the top of the lady's torso under the second flap, the bottom of the lady's torso under the third flap, and her legs and feet under the last flap. Invite children to close the bottom three flaps. Ask them to look at the lady's head and write on the inside of the adjoining flap a sentence that describes it. Have children repeat the steps with the remaining three flaps. Invite them to share with each other the "contents" of their alligator purse books.

Bear

A Teddy Bear's Picnic by _____	___eddy ___ear ate ___.
	___eddy ___ear ate ___.
___eddy ___ear ate ___.	___eddy ___ear ate ___.
___eddy ___ear ate ___.	___eddy ___ear is full!

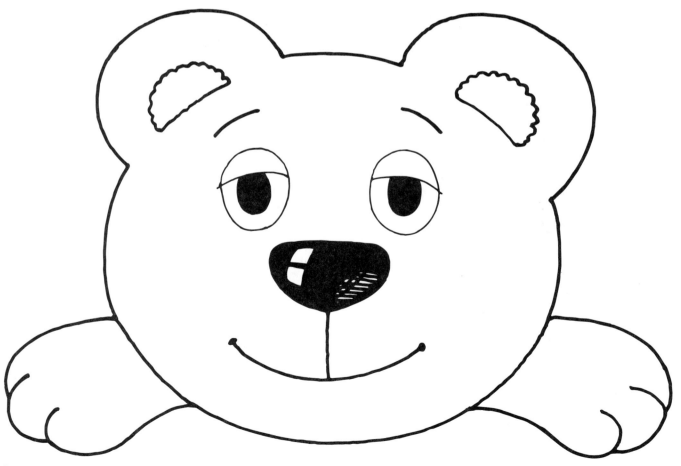

Materials

✓ scissors
✓ construction paper
✓ envelopes
✓ stapler
✓ small, flat objects
✓ crayons or markers

Envelope Books

Cut construction paper rectangle covers with the same dimensions as the envelopes, and give one to each child. Give each child three to five envelopes, and have children arrange them in a pile under the cover so the flaps face the back. Staple the left side of the pile to make a book. Invite children to insert an object in each envelope and draw a picture and write a descriptive sentence about each object on the front of the envelope.

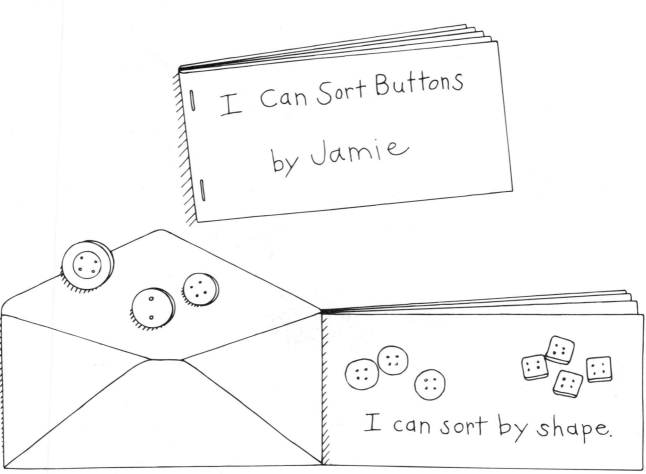

The Skin You Live In

Skill
✓ classification

Give each child three **envelopes,** and have children use the directions on page 9 to make an envelope book. Give each child a **feather, sequins** (scales), and a swatch of **fur fabric,** and have children glue the items to separate pages of their book and label the items. Give each child a set of **Animal Cards (page 12)** to color and cut apart. Invite children to name each animal and describe its skin. Ask children to write their name after the title and glue it to the cover of their book. Invite them to place each animal card in the envelope with the matching skin.

Sorting Buttons

Skills
✓ sorting
✓ writing descriptive sentences

Give each child three **envelopes,** and have children use the directions on page 9 to make an envelope book. Write *I Can Sort Buttons by ___* on the board, and ask children to write the title and their name on the cover of their book. Give each child a set of **buttons** to sort. Encourage children to draw on the first page one way they sorted their buttons and write a sentence that describes their illustration below it. Invite them to repeat the steps on the remaining two pages. Tell children to insert their buttons in the first envelope, and encourage them to take home their book to read and sort their buttons with friends or family members.

I Can Make Words

Give each child three **envelopes,** and have children use the directions on page 9 to make an envelope book. Give each child an **I Can Make Words reproducible (page 13)** to cut apart. Tell children to glue a rectangle to each envelope. Ask them to cut the remaining rectangles into squares to make letter tiles. Encourage children to think of a CVC word (e.g., *hat*), write each letter on a separate tile, and place the tiles in the first envelope. Invite children to repeat the steps with the remaining tiles and envelopes. Have them write their name after the title *I Can Make Words* and glue it to the cover of their book. Encourage children to exchange books. Ask them to remove the letter tiles from the first envelope and arrange them on the boxes to make a word. Tell children to replace the letters in the envelope and repeat the steps with the remaining envelopes.

Animal Cards

**What Skin
Do You Live In?**

by _____

I Can Make Words

I Can Make Words

by _____

Materials

✓ empty bathroom tissue rolls
✓ paint (optional)
✓ construction paper
✓ cash register tape or paper strips
✓ labels

Bathroom Tissue Roll Books

Invite each child to cover a bathroom tissue roll with paint or construction paper and add construction paper details. Encourage children to write a story on a piece of cash register tape or a paper strip, roll it up, and insert it inside the roll. Write the title and each child's name on a label, and give the label to the child to attach to the side of his or her roll.

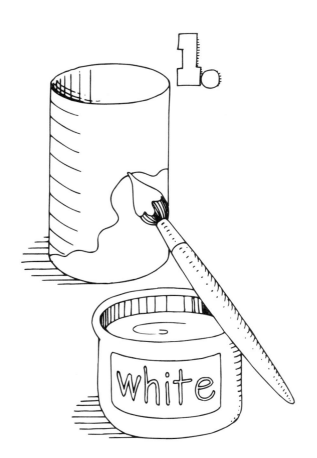

1.

white

2.

The Race to Space by Malcolm

Two rockets raced to space.

Insert rolled strip inside the roll.

A Butterfly Story

Give each child an **empty bathroom tissue roll.** Invite children to cover their roll with **yellow or silver construction paper or paint.** Give each child a **Butterfly reproducible (page 18)** to color and cut apart. Tell children to glue the wings to their roll. Help children hole-punch a hole at the top of their roll and insert a **pipe cleaner** to make antennae. Have children glue **wiggly eyes** or draw them below the antennae. Ask children to cut four leaves from **green construction paper.**

Give each child a piece of **cash register tape.** Show children how to position their tape vertically and glue a leaf at the top. Read aloud the sentences from the reproducible with children. Give each child a grain of **rice** and a piece of **curly pasta, rigatoni,** and **bow tie pasta.** Tell children to glue their grain of rice on the leaf to make an egg and glue the corresponding sentence below it. Ask children to repeat the steps with the remaining leaves, pasta (curly pasta/caterpillar, rigatoni/chrysalis, and bow tie pasta/butterfly), and sentences. Encourage children to use a **marker** to add feet and/or antennae to their caterpillar and butterfly. Invite them to read aloud their story. Tell children to roll their strip around a **pencil,** remove it, and place it inside their roll. Have children write their name after the title and glue it to the side of their butterfly (roll).

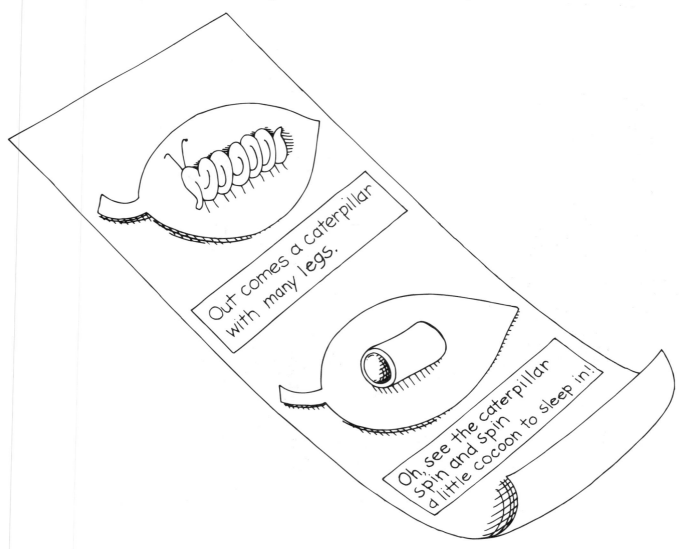

Out comes a caterpillar with many legs.

Oh, see the caterpillar spin and spin a little cocoon to sleep in!

Climbing Up the Coconut Tree

Skills
- ✓ tracking from top to bottom
- ✓ identifying letters
- ✓ arranging in alphabetical order
- ✓ using high-frequency words
- ✓ improving fluency

Copy a class set of the **Coconut Tree reproducible (page 19)** on **green construction paper.** Give each child an **empty bathroom tissue roll.** Invite children to cover their roll with **brown paint or construction paper.** Give each child a reproducible to cut apart. Tell children to glue the branches to the top of their roll. Ask children to cut small circles from brown paper (or use **brown pom-poms**) and glue them on the branches to make coconuts.

Read aloud *Chicka Chicka Boom Boom* by Bill Martin Jr. and John Archambault (Simon & Schuster), and discuss the activities of the letters in the story. Give each child a piece of **cash register tape** and a **magazine.** Invite children to find the letter *a*, cut it out, and glue it to the top of their cash register tape. Ask them to repeat this with letters *b* to *z*. Tell children to glue the chant from their reproducible to the bottom of their tape, and encourage them to read aloud their "story." Tell children to roll their strip around a **pencil,** remove it, and place it inside their roll. Have children write their name after the title and glue it to the side of their tree (roll).

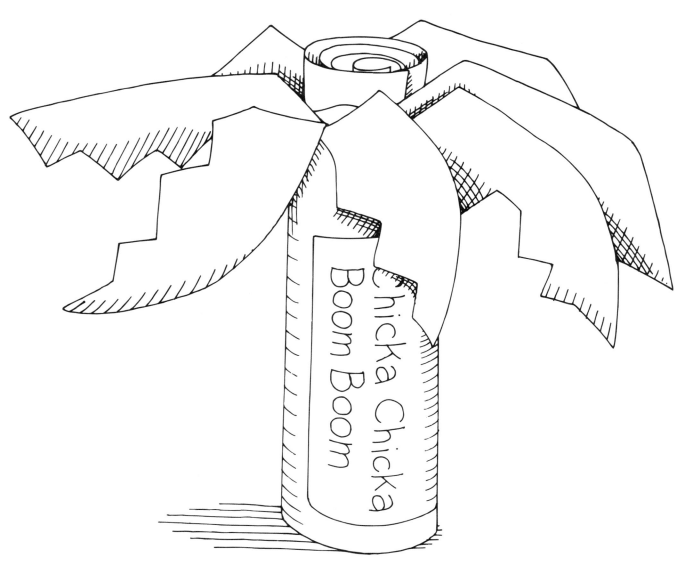

Mouse Mixes Paint

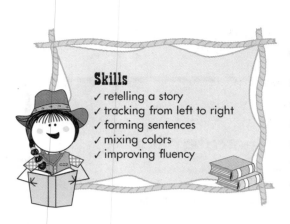
Copy a class set of the **Mouse reproducible (page 20)** on **pink construction paper.** Give each child an **empty bathroom tissue roll.** Invite children to cover their roll with **white construction paper or paint.** Give each child a Mouse reproducible to cut apart. Tell children to glue the feet, tail, nose, and ears to their roll. Ask children to cut small strips of **black paper** and glue them under the nose to make whiskers.

Read aloud *Mouse Paint* **by Ellen Stoll Walsh (Harcourt).** Ask children to retell the story. Give each child a piece of **cash register tape.** Show children how to position it horizontally and glue their mouse cutout to the left side. Tell children to find the word cards *Mouse, danced,* and *in* and glue them in order beside their mouse. Invite children to use **red and yellow paint** to make two separate circles after their mouse. Encourage them to mix the red and yellow paint to make a third orange circle. Tell children to repeat the steps with another set of words and **blue and yellow paint.** Ask children to name what color the blue and yellow paint will make before they mix them together. Tell children to find the word cards *Mouse, made, a,* and *rainbow* and glue them in order after the green circle. Ask children to use all six colors of paint to paint a rainbow. Invite them to read aloud their story. Tell children to roll their strip around a **pencil,** remove it, and place it inside their roll. Have children write their name after the title and glue it to the side of their mouse (roll).

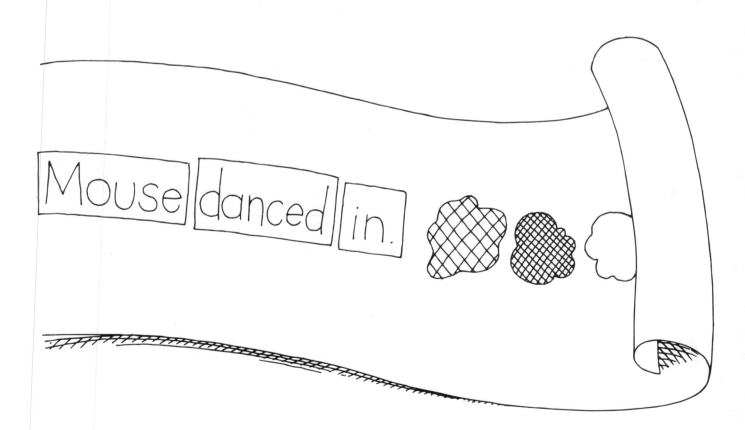

Butterfly

The Life Cycle of a Butterfly

by _____

First comes the butterfly
who lays an egg.

Out comes a caterpillar
with many legs.

Oh, see the caterpillar
spin and spin
a little cocoon to sleep in!

Oh, oh, oh! Look and see!
Oh, oh, oh! Look and see!
Out of the cocoon—
my, oh, my—
out comes a beautiful butterfly!

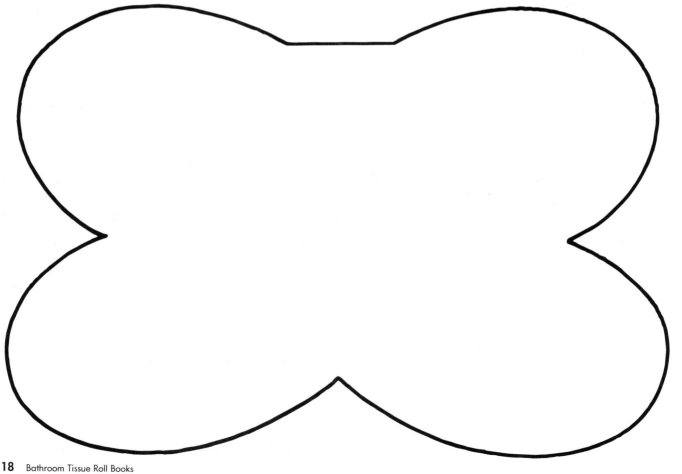

Coconut Tree

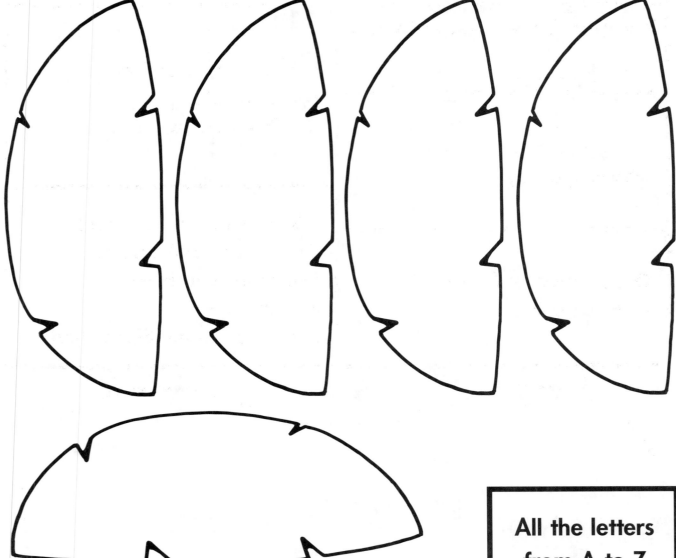

All the letters
from A to Z
climbing up the
coconut tree!

All the Letters
Up the Coconut Tree
by _____

Mouse

Mouse Paint
by _____

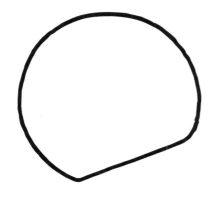

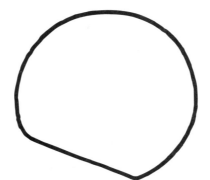

1	**danced**	**in**	**Mouse**
2	**in**	**Mouse**	**danced**
3	**a** **made**	**Mouse**	**rainbow**

Plastic Bottle Books

Materials

✓ small, empty plastic soda bottles
✓ small theme-related objects
✓ paper
✓ rubber bands
✓ yarn or curling ribbon
✓ labels
✓ stapler (optional)
✓ construction paper (optional)
✓ hole punch (optional)

Collect small plastic soda bottles, and clean them out. Give each child a bottle and small theme-related items to place inside it. Ask children to write a story on a piece of paper, roll it up, and place a rubber band around it. Have children tie one end of a piece of yarn or curling ribbon to the rubber band and the other end to the neck of the bottle. Tell them to insert their paper in their bottle. Write the title and each child's name on a label, and have children attach their label to the side of their bottle. Or, staple together several pieces of paper under a construction paper cover, and invite children to write a story inside it. Hole-punch a corner of the book, tie a piece of yarn or curling ribbon through the hole, and tie the other end to the top of the bottle.

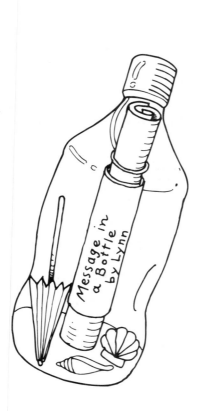

Message in a Bottle by Lynn

What Can Float? by Paulo

Message in a Bottle

Skills
✓ rhyming
✓ writing sentences

Invite children to help you write a rhyme or story about the ocean like the one shown below.

1,1 Whales have fun.
2, 2 Starfish for you.
3, 3 Fish in the sea.
4, 4 Shells galore.
5, 5 Dolphins dive!

Write the rhyme or story on a piece of **chart paper,** and explain to children the strategies you use to spell the words as you write them. For example, say *I know that **fun** rhymes with **sun,** so I'll change the **s** to an **f.** Or, **Starfish** has two words in it—**star** and **fish.** Invite children to make up their own rhyme or copy the class poem on a piece of paper and illustrate it. Give each child an **empty plastic soda bottle.** Write *Message in a Bottle* and each child's name on a **label,** and have children attach their label to the side of their bottle. Invite children to place **sand, small shells,** and a **cocktail umbrella** in their bottle and place **ocean stickers** on the outside to decorate it. Show children how to roll up their paper and place a **rubber band** around it. Have them tie one end of a piece of **yarn or curling ribbon** to the rubber band and the other end to the neck of the bottle. Tell children to insert their paper in their bottle. Tell them to replace the cap on their bottle and exchange bottles with a classmate to read.

What Is in the Grass?

Skill
✓ writing descriptive sentences

Give each child five **index cards** to staple together, and write *What Is in the Grass?* on the board. Have children copy it and write their name on the cover of their book. Give each child an **empty plastic soda bottle,** and tell children to fill it with **plastic or paper grass.** Have children insert a **small object (e.g., plastic spider ring, marble)** in the bottle. Tell them to write a sentence that describes the object (e.g., *It is round.*) on each of the first three pages of their book. Have children write *It is a _____!* and the name of the object on the last page. Encourage them to illustrate their book. Hole-punch the top corner of each book, tie one end of a piece of **curling ribbon** through the hole, and tie the other end to the top of the bottle. Tell children to replace the cap on their bottle and exchange bottles with a classmate to read.

Does It Attract?

Skills
✓ exploring magnets
✓ reading high-
frequency words

Give each child a **Does It Attract? reproducible (page 24)** to cut apart. Have children write their name after the title and staple the five other pages behind it. Give each child an **empty plastic soda bottle,** and ask children to place **five metal objects and five nonmetal objects** inside their bottle. Give each child a **magnet,** and have children use it to determine which items attract and which do not. Tell children to write on each page of their book the name of one object that attracts and one that does not on each line and draw a picture of both objects in the space provided. Help children hole-punch the top corner of their book, tie one end of a piece of **curling ribbon** through the hole, and tie the other end to the top of their bottle. Tell them to replace the cap on their bottle and exchange bottles with a classmate to read.

What Can Float?

Skills
✓ exploring buoyancy
✓ reading high-
frequency words

Give each child a **What Can Float? reproducible (page 25)** to cut apart. Have children write their name after the title and staple the five other pages behind it. Give each child an **empty plastic soda bottle,** and ask children to place **five objects that can float and five that cannot** inside their bottle. Have children fill their bottle with water, replace the cap, and determine which items float and which do not. Tell them to write the name of one object that floats and one that does not on each line and draw a picture of both objects in the space provided. Help children hole-punch the top corner of their book, tie one end of a piece of **curling ribbon** through the hole, and tie the other end to the top of the bottle. Ask them to exchange bottles with a classmate to read.

Does It Attract?

Does It Attract?

by _____

A _____
does attract.
A _____
does not attract.

A _____
does attract.
A _____
does not attract.

A _____
does attract.
A _____
does not attract.

A _____
does attract.
A _____
does not attract.

A _____
does attract.
A _____
does not attract.

What Can Float?

What Can Float?

by _____

A _____
can float.

A _____
can not float.

A _____
can float.

A _____
can not float.

A _____
can float.

A _____
can not float.

A _____
can float.

A _____
can not float.

A _____
can float.

A _____
can not float.

Plastic Egg Books

Materials

✓ cash register tape
✓ pencils
✓ plastic eggs
✓ permanent marker

Give each child a piece of cash register tape. Invite children to write a story on their register tape. Show them how to roll their strip around a pencil, remove the pencil, and insert the paper coil inside a plastic egg. Use a permanent marker to write the title of each story and each child's name on the outside of his or her egg.

See the egg.

Egg to Chick
by Anton

The egg cracks.

ABCD

Sing the ABCs with Me
by Megan

Egg to Chick

Give each child a piece of **cash register tape** and a **Life Cycle reproducible (page 28)** to cut apart. Show children how to arrange their register tape vertically and glue the sentence that describes the first part of the life cycle of a chick near the top. Tell them to glue the picture of the egg above this sentence. Have children repeat the steps to arrange and glue the remaining sentences and pictures in order on their tape. As an option, have children use a **yellow stamp pad** to make thumbprint chicks and a **marker** to add eyes, a beak, and legs. Tell them to roll their strip around a **pencil,** remove it, and place it inside a **plastic egg.** Use a **permanent marker** to write *Egg to Chick* and each child's name on the outside of his or her egg.

See the chick.

The chick is born.

Alphabet Egg Books

Give each child a piece of **cash register tape.** Invite children to use a **marker or alphabet stamps** to add the letters from A to Z on their register tape. Tell them to roll their strip around a **pencil,** remove it, and place it inside a **plastic egg.** Use a **permanent marker** to write *Sing the ABCs with Me* and each child's name on the outside of his or her egg.

Life Cycle

See the egg.
The egg cracks.
See the chick.
The chick is born.

Materials

✓ cash register tape
✓ pencils
✓ film canisters
✓ labels

Film Canister Books

Give each child a piece of cash register tape. Invite children to write a story on their register tape. Show them how to roll their strip around a pencil, remove it, and place it inside a film canister. Write the title of each story and each child's name on a label, and have children attach their label to the side of their canister.

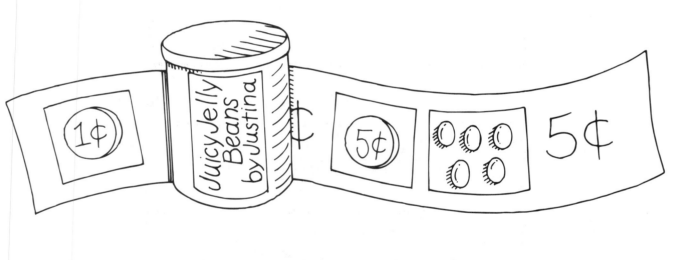

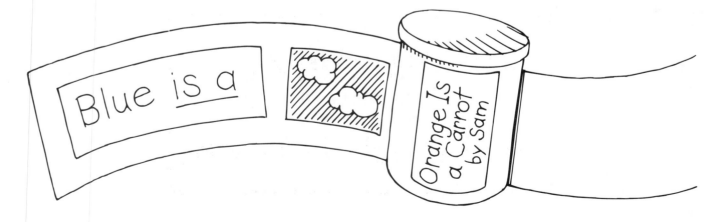

Bean Counters

Give each child a piece of **cash register tape** and a **Jelly Beans reproducible (page 31)** to color and cut apart. Ask children to position their register tape horizontally and glue the chant from their reproducible to the left side. Tell them to locate the penny and glue it beside the chant. Tell children to find one jelly bean, glue it beside the penny, and write *1¢* beside it. Encourage them to repeat these steps with the nickel, the dime, and the quarter. Tell children to roll their strip around a **pencil,** remove it, and insert it in a **film canister.** Write *Juicy Jelly Beans* and each child's name on a **label,** and have children attach their label to the side of their canister.

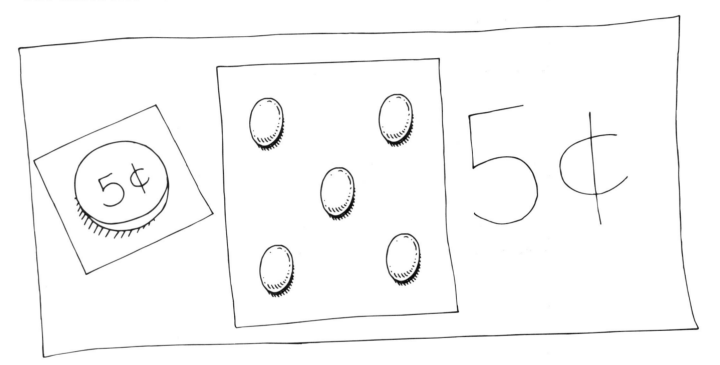

Orange Is a Carrot

Review the high-frequency words *is* and *a*, and write them on the board. Give each child an **Orange Is a Carrot reproducible (page 32),** review the color words and names of the pictures with the class, and have children cut apart their paper. Tell children to locate the sentence strip that begins with *Orange* and use an orange **marker** to write *is a* on the blank lines. Give each child a piece of **cash register tape.** Show children how to position their tape horizontally, and have them glue their sentence to the left side. Ask children to find the picture of something that is orange, color it, and glue it beside their sentence. Have them repeat these steps with yellow, green, brown, purple, blue, black, and red. Invite children to read aloud their completed poem. Give each child a **film canister.** Tell children to roll their strip around a **pencil,** remove it, and place it in their film canister. Write *Orange Is a Carrot* and each child's name on a **label,** and have children attach their label to the side of their canister.

Jelly Beans

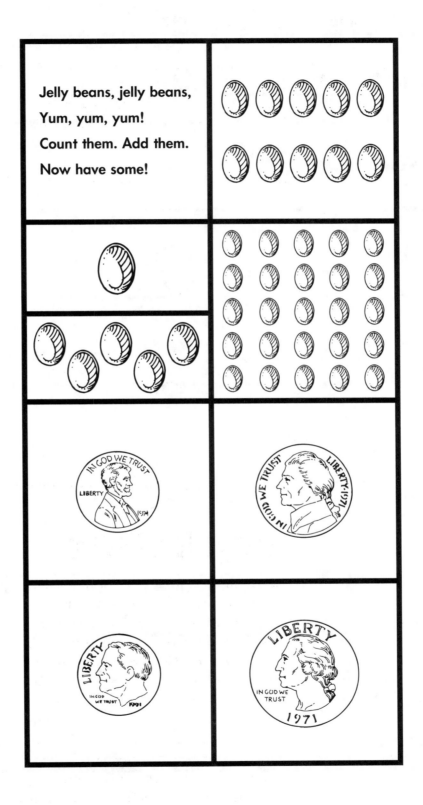

Jelly beans, jelly beans,
Yum, yum, yum!
Count them. Add them.
Now have some!

Orange Is a Carrot

Orange ___ ___	Green ___ ___
Yellow ___ ___	Blue ___ ___
Purple ___ ___	Black ___ ___
Brown ___ ___	Red ___ ___

Paper Plate Books

Materials

✓ scissors
✓ paper plates
✓ brass fasteners
✓ crayons or markers
✓ small construction paper rectangles
✓ hole punch
✓ ribbon

Use scissors to carefully make a hole in the center of two paper plates, and give a set of plates and a brass fastener to each child. Have children insert a brass fastener through both holes to connect the plates. Tell children to cut a small wedge from the top plate and write the first part of a story in the uncovered section of the bottom plate. Show children how to rotate the top plate to a blank section and write the next part of their story in the space. Ask them to repeat these steps to write in each section of the bottom plate. Have children decorate the top plate to coordinate with the theme of their story. Invite them to write the title of their story on a construction paper rectangle, hole-punch one corner, tie one end of a ribbon through it, and tie the other end to the brass fastener.

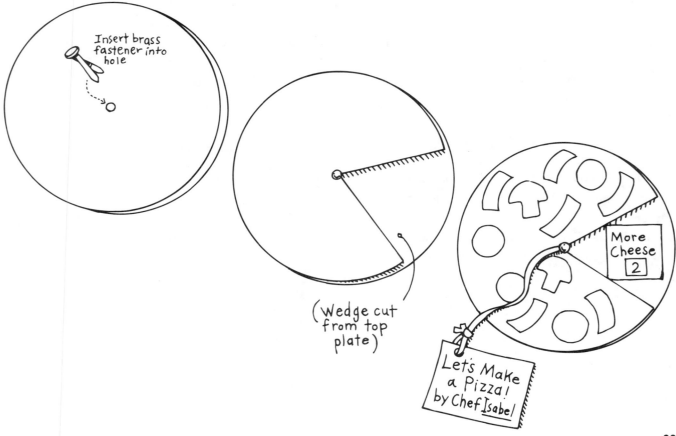

Insert brass fastener into hole

(Wedge cut from top plate)

More Cheese 2

Let's Make a Pizza! by Chef Isabel

Let's Make a Pizza!

Skills
✓ comparing quantities
✓ counting

Use the directions on page 33 to help children make a paper plate book. Invite children to cover the top **paper plate** with **brown paint or construction paper.** Have children cut out small circles from **red, brown, and black construction paper** to make pepperoni, tomatoes, sausages, and olives; strips of **yellow, white, and green construction paper** to make pineapple chunks, cheese, and peppers; and squares of **pink construction paper** to make pieces of ham. Give each child a **Pizza reproducible (page 35)** to cut apart. Tell children to cut a small wedge from the top plate and glue an "ingredients" square in the uncovered section of the bottom plate. Show children how to rotate the top plate to a blank section and glue another square in the space. Encourage children to repeat these steps with the six remaining squares. Tell them to use a **marker** to write a number from one to ten in each box. Ask children to read each box and glue on top of their pizza that quantity of ingredients. Have them write their name after the title and glue it to a **construction paper rectangle.** Ask children to glue their **individual class photo** or draw their face on the head of the chef. Help children hole-punch the top corner, tie one end of a piece of **curling ribbon** through it, and tie the other end to the **brass fastener.**

A Family of Fish

Skills
✓ manipulating beginning and ending sounds
✓ sequencing

Read aloud the chant on the **Fish reproducible (page 36),** and invite children to reread it with you. Use the directions on page 33 to help children make a paper plate book. Tell children to cut a wedge from their top **paper plate** and glue it to the end opposite the mouth to make a tail. Invite children to glue a **wiggly eye** above the mouth and glue **small construction paper squares** to their plate to make scales. Give each child a Fish reproducible to cut apart. Tell children to glue the smallest fish in the uncovered section of the bottom plate. Invite children to rotate the top plate and glue the next biggest fish to the bottom plate. Encourage them to repeat these steps with the remaining pieces. Ask children to write their name after the title and glue it to a larger construction paper square. Help them hole-punch the top corner, tie one end of a piece of **curling ribbon** through it, and tie the other end to the **brass fastener.** To extend learning, challenge children to change the beginning or ending sound of *Do-do-do-do-do-do* to make new sounds, such as *Bo-bo-bo-bo-bo-bo* or *Da-da-da-da-da-da.*

Baby Fish
Do-do-do-do-do-do

Pizza

Let's Make
a Pizza!

by Chef _____

More pepperoni	Less olives	More pineapple	Less ham
☐	☐	☐	☐
More cheese	Less sausage	More peppers	Less tomatoes
☐	☐	☐	☐

Fish

A Family of Fish
by

_____

Sister Fish
Do-do-do-do-do-do

Baby Fish
Do-do-do-do-do-do

Mommy Fish
Do-do-do-do-do-do

Brother Fish
Do-do-do-do-do-do

Daddy Fish
Do-do-do-do-do-do

Napkin Books

✓ heavy-duty, decorated
   paper napkins
✓ paper
✓ scissors
✓ stapler
✓ marker

Give each child a paper napkin and several pieces of paper. Have children cut their paper to match the size and shape of their napkin and then staple the papers inside it to make a book. Use a marker to write the title of each story and each child's name on the cover of his or her book.

Insert pages into open napkin.

Friends I Love by A.J.

Friends I Love Phone Books

Skills
✓ arranging in alphabetical order
✓ reading numerals

Use **Valentine's Day napkins** and the directions on page 37 to help children make a five-page napkin book. Explain to children that Valentine's Day is a good time to use a telephone to call a friend or family member to say we love them. Invite children to make a phone book that features five of their classmates' phone numbers. Photocopy **individual class photos,** and have children glue one photo on each page of their book, or have children draw a picture of five different friends on separate pages of their book. Have children write the name of each classmate and his or her phone number below the corresponding picture. Use a **marker** to write *Friends I Love Phone Book* and each child's name on his or her cover. As an option, encourage children to organize their classmates in alphabetical order. Or, invite children to use **inoperable telephones and cellular phones** and the numbers in their phone book to "call" their classmates.

My Super Snowman

Skills
✓ sequencing
✓ counting
✓ improving fluency
✓ reading number words

Invite children to name the features of a snowman, such as a carrot nose and a raisin smile. Use **paper napkins decorated with snowmen or snowflakes** and the directions on page 37 to help children make a six-page book. Give each child a **My Super Snowman reproducible (page 39)** to cut apart. Ask children to arrange their strips in order and glue one sentence frame to the bottom of each page of their book. Have them draw a carrot nose or cut one from **orange construction paper** and glue it to the first page. Ask children to turn to the next page of their book and draw two mittens or cut them from construction paper and glue them above the sentence. Have children repeat the process on the remaining pages to show three stripes (on a hat), four **dried black beans** (for a raisin smile), and five **small buttons.** Encourage children to read their books to each other to practice fluency.

My snowman has two mittens.

My Super Snowman

My snowman has one carrot nose.

My snowman has two mittens.

My snowman has three stripes.

My snowman has four raisins.

My snowman has five buttons.

Do you like my snowman?

Food Package Books

Ask children to save food wrappers from their lunches or collect other food packages to use as book covers. Have children clean their wrappers or packages and cut them to make book covers. Tell children to cut paper to fit their cover and attach it with staples, yarn, or other fasteners. Help children write the title of their story and their name on a label and then attach it to the cover of their book.

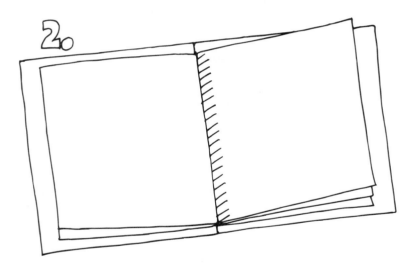

Candy Wrapper Books

Give each child a **small bag of of M & M's®, Skittles®, or other small candy** with several pieces that are different colors. Ask children to cut off one end of their bag and carefully pour the contents on a flat surface. Use the directions on page 40 to help children make a book cover. Give each child a **Candy Patterns reproducible (page 43)** to cut apart. Tell children to arrange their pages in order in a pile and staple them inside their cover. Help children read the sentence on each page and follow the directions. Tell children to draw how they sorted and patterned their candy and write the number of pieces they counted. On the last page, have children draw and write the number word for the number of pieces they ate.

I patterned.
3

Cereal Box Books

Give each child a piece of **paper.** Write on the board *We like _____,* and ask children to copy the frame on the bottom of their paper. Invite children to complete the frame with a food they like. Ask them to find a picture of their food in a **magazine,** cut it out, and glue it to the top of their paper. Use a **craft knife** to cut three edges of the front panel of an **empty cereal box** to make a "door." Staple children's papers together to make a book, and glue the last page of it to the inside back of the cereal box. As a variation, give each child an **empty individual-serving-size box of cereal** to use to make a book of foods he or she likes.

Skills

✓ using elements of a story
✓ adding detail to writing

Snack Chip Bag Books

Use the directions on page 40 to help children make a snack chip bag book. Discuss with children elements of a story, including character and setting. Invite them to write and illustrate in their book a story that features an interesting setting and characters. As an option, invite children to illustrate their story first and then write a sentence to describe each picture. Encourage children to add detail to their stories.

Skills

✓ using word family words
✓ rhyming

Mint Candy Box Books

Give each child a **Word Families reproducible (page 44)** to color and cut apart. Have children glue their song to a **2.5" x 4.5" (6.3 cm x 11.5 cm) construction paper rectangle** and glue the rectangle to the top of a **metal mint candy box.** Give each child a piece of **cash register tape** to position horizontally. Invite children to choose two picture cards and glue them on the left side of their register tape. Help children write the word for each picture beneath it and write *and* between the words (e.g., *cat and hat*). Ask children to repeat the steps with the remaining picture cards. Tell children to write *The -At Family* at the end of their strip, fold it accordion-style into the box, and replace the lid. To extend learning, invite children to choose a different word family, change the words of the song, and make a new mint box book.

Candy Patterns

_____'s

Candy Book

_____'s
Candy Book

I counted.

1

I patterned.

3

I sorted.

2

I ate!

4

Word Families

Word Families

by _____

(sing to the tune of "For He's a Jolly Good Fellow")

I can sing the "at" family.
I can sing the "at" family.
I can sing the "at" family.
Come and sing with me!

Paper Lunch Sack Books

Materials

✓ paper lunch sacks
✓ art supplies (e.g., crayons, markers, glitter, ribbon, stickers)
✓ scissors
✓ paper
✓ stapler
✓ construction paper (optional)
✓ glue (optional)

Give each child a paper lunch sack. Invite children to use art supplies to decorate their sack. Cut pieces of paper in half, and give a few to each child to staple together to make a book. Encourage children to write in their book and then place it inside their bag.

Another option is to have children cut and fold their sack to make a box. Ask children to open their sack and cut three-fourths of the way down one of the "seams." Tell children to cut on the remaining three seams. Have them use the scissors to horizontally cut off three panels (the front and two sides) and fold the remaining side of the sack down to make a lid for their paper box book. Invite children to cut a face from construction paper and glue it to the top of the lid and the side below it to make a mouth, or have them use art supplies to decorate the book in other ways.

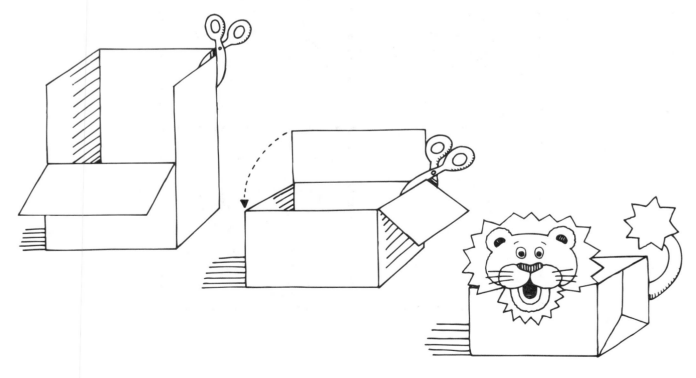

Lion's Lunch Box

Use the directions on page 45 to help children make a lunch box book out of a **paper lunch sack.** Give each child a **Lion and Fish reproducible (page 47)** to color and cut apart. Tell children to glue the lion's head to the top of their box, its mouth below the head, and the tail on the back. Determine the number of fish you would like children to use in their subtraction practice, and have them line up this number of fish on their desk. Give each child a **One Hungry Lion reproducible (page 48)** to color. Tell children to cut apart the pages and staple them together in order. Read with children the rhyme on the first page, and insert the number you selected in the blank space. Have children place the same number of fish in their box and count the number that remains. Help them write at the bottom of their page a number sentence to show what they did. Invite children to repeat the steps until they have completed each page in their book. Then, have children staple their book below the lid of their box, place any remaining fish in the box, and take it home for some extra reading and subtraction practice.

The Seed Song

Give each child a **paper lunch sack.** Invite children to decorate their sack to look like a garden. Tell children to use **sponges** to paint brown dirt at the bottom, a blue sky at the top, and a yellow sun in the top corner. As an option, have children glue **ground coffee** to the bottom for dirt. Give each child **dried lima beans** to glue on the dirt to make carrot seeds. Have children cut carrots from **orange construction paper** and glue them above the seeds. Give each child **The Seed Song reproducible (page 49)** to color and cut apart. Teach children to sing the song to the tune of "Mary Had a Little Lamb." Have children place their cards in sequential order and then place them in their sack. Tell children to write their name on their sack and take it home to read to a family member.

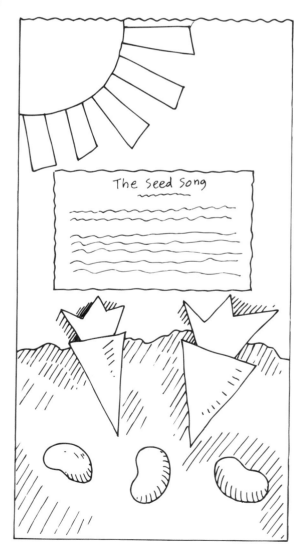

The Seed Song

Lion and Fish

One Hungry Lion

One Hungry Lion

by _____

(sing to the tune of "One Elephant Went out to Play")

One hungry lion went out to play
On a sunny summer day.
It had such an appetite
That it ate _____ fish for dinner
    that night!

One hungry lion went out to play
On a sunny summer day.
It had such an appetite
That it ate _____ fish for dinner
    that night!

One hungry lion went out to play
On a sunny summer day.
It had such an appetite
That it ate _____ fish for dinner
    that night!

One hungry lion went out to play
On a sunny summer day.
It had such an appetite
That it ate _____ fish for dinner
    that night!

One hungry lion went out to play
On a sunny summer day.
It had such an appetite
That it ate _____ fish for dinner
    that night!

The Seed Song

(sing to the tune of "Mary Had a Little Lamb")

I am planting little seeds, little seeds, little seeds.
I am planting little seeds with a /s/, /s/, /s/, /s/, /s/.

I am sprinkling my seeds with water,
my seeds with water, my seeds with water.
I am sprinkling my seeds with water
with a /w/, /w/, /w/, /w/, /w/.

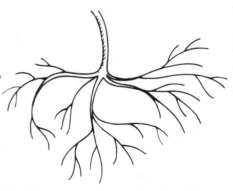

I am watching the growing roots,
the growing roots, the growing roots.
I am watching the growing roots
with an /r/, /r/, /r/, /r/, /r/.

I am eating crunchy carrots,
crunchy carrots, crunchy carrots.
I am eating crunchy carrots
with a /c/, /c/, /c/, /c/, /c/.

Grocery Sack Books

✓ paper grocery sacks
✓ scissors
✓ stapler
✓ paper
✓ Velcro® tape
✓ hole punch
✓ pipe cleaners

Give each child a grocery sack. Show children how to use scissors to cut along the "seam" at the bottom along three sides. Tell children to place their sack in a landscape orientation with the open flap to the right and flatten it. Have children fold the left side to the cut edge of the right side and open it again to make a crease. Ask them to staple several pieces of paper inside their book and fold over the flap to make a cover. Have each child use Velcro tape to attach the folded side and the back of the flap to keep the cover closed. Help children hole-punch three holes along the creased side. Ask them to cut a pipe cleaner into three pieces, insert one piece through each hole, and twist each one closed. Have children write a title and their name on the front cover of their book.

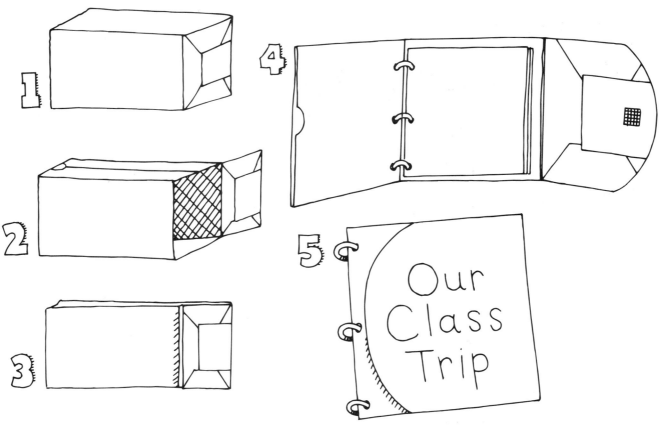

Field Trip Journals

Give each child a **grocery sack book (see page 50)** to take on a class field trip. Encourage children to collect materials (e.g., leaves, pamphlets) and place them in the pocket/flap of their book. Invite children to draw and label on the pages of their book pictures of things they see on their trip. Encourage them to also draw in their book a map of the place they are visiting or use the pages to record questions to ask upon their return to the classroom. As an option, ask children to write *Our Class Trip* and their name on the cover of their book. Invite children to compare with each other notes about their trip.

Homework Journals

Give each child a **grocery sack book (see page 50)** to take on a family weekend outing or vacation. Encourage children to collect materials (e.g., photographs, ticket stubs) and place them in the pocket/flap of their book. Invite children to draw and label on the pages of their book pictures of things they see on their outing. Encourage them to also draw in their book a map of the place they are visiting or use the pages to record information they would like to share with the class. As an option, ask children to write *My Weekend Adventures* and their name on the cover of their book. Invite children to share details of their book with the class.

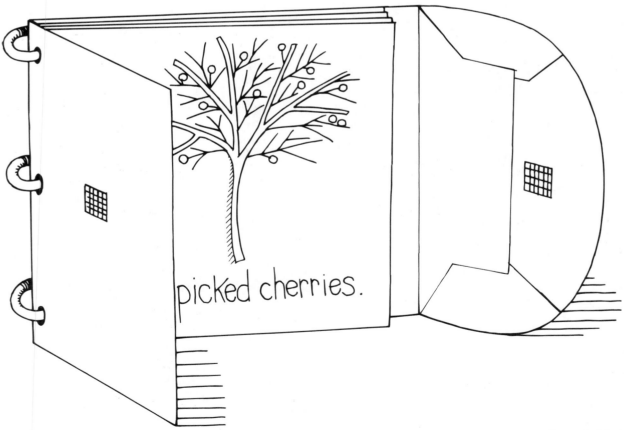

picked cherries.

Materials

✓ resealable plastic
   bags
✓ crayons or markers
✓ index cards or paper
✓ stapler
✓ tape (masking or
   colored)
✓ assorted small, flat
   objects

Resealable Plastic Bag Books

Give each child several resealable bags of the same size. Ask children to arrange the bags in a pile. Invite children to write and draw on index cards or pieces of paper, place them in separate bags, and staple the bags together along the resealable side. Help children cover the staples with colored or masking tape. Or, tell children to staple together the opposite end, cover the staples with tape and insert objects and captions in separate bags after their book is bound. As an option, ask an adult volunteer to prepare in advance a five-page book for each child to use in an activity.

Seasonal Books

Skills
✓ writing sentences
✓ observing seasons

Invite each child to bring in four **small objects** that represent a particular season, such as a leaf, a pumpkin seed, a magazine cutout of food, and an apple sticker for fall. Give each child five **small resealable bags,** an **unlined index card,** and four **white labels.** Have children write the name of the season in the frame _____ *Is* on their index card and place it in the first bag. Tell children to place one of their objects in the second bag, write on a label a sentence to describe it, and attach the label to the bag. Ask children to repeat these steps with the three remaining bags. Help them staple together their bags at the resealable end and bind the edge with **masking or colored tape.** Encourage children to read their books to each other.

ABC Baggie Books

Skills
- ✓ identifying beginning sounds
- ✓ identifying letters of the alphabet
- ✓ identifying uppercase and lowercase letters

Use the directions on page 52 to make several five-page plastic bag books that are bound along the edge opposite the resealable edge. Give each small group of children a book and five **5" x 6" (12.5 cm x 15 cm) construction paper rectangles.** Tell children to write the capital and lowercase version of a letter on a rectangle, place it in their first bag, and reseal it. Invite children to cut out **magazine pictures** of items that begin with the letter. (Or, have children use **stickers.**) Tell children to glue their pictures to separate construction paper rectangles and place them in the four remaining bags.

Opposites

Skill
- ✓ identifying opposites

Say *big*, and ask children to name the opposite (i.e., *small*). Write *big* and *small* on a piece of **chart paper.** Invite children to name other pairs of opposites (e.g., *hard/soft, short/long, rough/smooth*), and write them on the paper. Use the directions on page 52 to make for each child a six-page book that is bound along the edge opposite the resealable edge. Give each child five **small, flat objects (e.g., buttons, feathers, coins)** and an **Opposites reproducible (page 55)** to cut apart. Tell children to write their name after the title and place it in their first bag. Have children glue an object on each remaining page. Encourage them to use the list of opposite words or think of others to complete the sentence frames. Then, have children place each page in a separate bag. Staple together the resealable end of each bag, and cover the staples with **masking or colored tape.**

Is it _soft_ ? No.
Is it _hard_ ? Yes.

Opposites

Opposites

by _____

Is it _____? No.
Is it _____? Yes.

Is it _____? No.
Is it _____? Yes.

Is it _____? No.
Is it _____? Yes.

Is it _____? No.
Is it _____? Yes.

Is it _____? No.
Is it _____? Yes.

Paper Doll Books

Materials

✓ 9" x 12"
(23 cm x 30.5 cm)
construction paper
✓ scissors
✓ glue
✓ art supplies (e.g.,
crayons, markers,
paint/paintbrush,
glitter, ribbon)
✓ stapler
✓ paper

Show children how to fold a piece of construction paper into eight equal sections. Have children place their paper in a landscape position and cut out the bottom left and bottom right sections for later use. Show them how to fold the top right and top left sections inward to make a "jacket." Tell children to glue one of the section cutouts behind each side of the jacket to make arms. Ask children to trace a circle on construction paper, cut it out, and glue it to the top to make a head. Encourage them to add paper hands and feet. Invite children to use art supplies to add facial features and details to the clothing. Have them open the jacket and staple paper behind it to make a book. Tell children to write a title and their name on the front of the jacket.

Patterns All around Me Doll

Skills

✓ patterning
✓ using sight words
✓ improving fluency

Discuss with children how to use letters to describe a pattern, such as ABAB, ABCABC, or AABAAB. Ask children to describe patterns they see on their clothing. Use the directions on page 56 to help children make a paper doll book. Invite children to use **crayons, markers, or paint** to create a different pattern on the pants, jacket, and shoes of their paper doll, and ask them to add features to the face. As an option, have children glue **crinkle paper or yarn** to the head to make hair. Give each child a **Pattern Pages reproducible (page 58)** to cut apart and staple in order beneath the jacket of their doll. Review the high-frequency words *on* and *my,* and write them on the board. Tell children to use the words to complete the sentences on the pages of their book. Have children draw patterns to illustrate their sentences, and encourage them to use letters (e.g., ABAB) to describe their patterns. Ask children to write *Patterns All Around Me* and their name on their doll's jacket.

Who Am I?

Discuss with children things about them that make them special. Use the directions on page 56 to help children make a paper doll book. Invite them to use **crayons, markers, or paint** to decorate their dolls to look like themselves. Give each child a **Who Am I? reproducible (page 59)** to cut apart and staple in order beneath the jacket of their doll. Review the high-frequency words *I, have, who,* and *am,* and write them on the board. Tell children to use the words to complete the sentences on the pages of their book. Have them illustrate their sentences. As an option, invite children to glue their **individual class photo** above the last sentence. Display children's dolls on a bulletin board titled *Who Am I?*

Skills

✓ improving self-esteem
✓ using high-frequency and descriptive words
✓ writing sentences
✓ improving fluency

Pattern Pages

Patterns _____ shirt.
1

Patterns _____ pants.
3

Patterns _____ buttons.
2

Patterns _____ shoes.
4

Who Am I?

_____ 1 _____ eyes.

_____ 2 _____ hair.

_____ 3 _____ Who am I? _____ years old.

_____ 4 _____ !

Bookmaking Bonanza © 2004 Creative Teaching Press

✓ copy or construction
   paper of any size
✓ stapler

Step Books

Show children how to place a piece of paper over another piece of paper so that a 1" (2.5 cm) margin appears at the bottom. Have children place another piece over the top piece, leaving a 1" margin at the bottom again. Tell them to hold their papers securely in place and then fold the top piece of paper over so that a 1" margin appears at the bottom. Tell children to repeat this with the remaining two pieces of paper. Ask them to staple the papers along the top crease. As an option, give children additional pieces of paper to add "steps," or have them turn their book sideways to change the orientation. Invite children to write their story along the bottom edge of each flap so that it can be read without turning the pages. Encourage them to illustrate each sentence in the space above it.

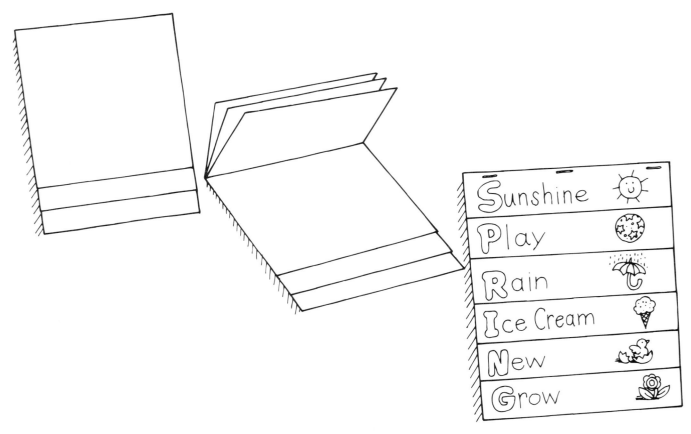

Steps to Making a Snowman

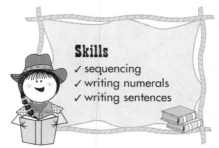

Skills
✓ sequencing
✓ writing numerals
✓ writing sentences

Use the directions on page 60 to help children make a six-page step book out of **white construction paper.** Give each child a **Snowman reproducible (page 62).** Show children how to place their snowman over their book (stapled edge at top), and give them a **paper clip** to hold their papers in place. Tell children to cut along the lines and through the pages of the step book to create a shape book. Invite children to draw a hat and face on the top page of their book. Ask them to name the steps they could follow to make a snowman. Have children flip to the second page of their book and draw a circle at the top. Ask them to write *1.* and a sentence that explains how a snowman begins with a large snowball at the bottom of their page. Have children flip to the next page and draw a smaller circle on top of a larger circle. Tell children to write *2.* and a sentence that explains that a smaller snowball goes on top of the larger one at the bottom of their page. Invite children to repeat the steps to write steps three through five on the remaining pages.

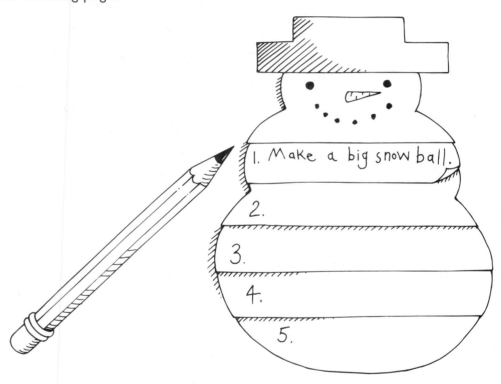

Thanks!

Skills
✓ identifying beginning sounds
✓ identifying letters
✓ tracking from top to bottom

Use the directions on page 60 to help children make a six-page step book out of **orange, yellow, or brown construction paper.** Have children cut out a triangle from construction paper and glue it to the top of their book to make a "roof." Write *I Am Thankful for . . .* and each child's name on the roof of his or her book. Write *T H A N K S* on the board, and have children write one letter along the edge on each page of their book. Give children **magazines and newspapers,** and ask them to cut out a picture of a food or an object that begins with each letter of *thanks.* Tell them to glue each picture beside the corresponding letter and write the name of the word next to it.

Snowman

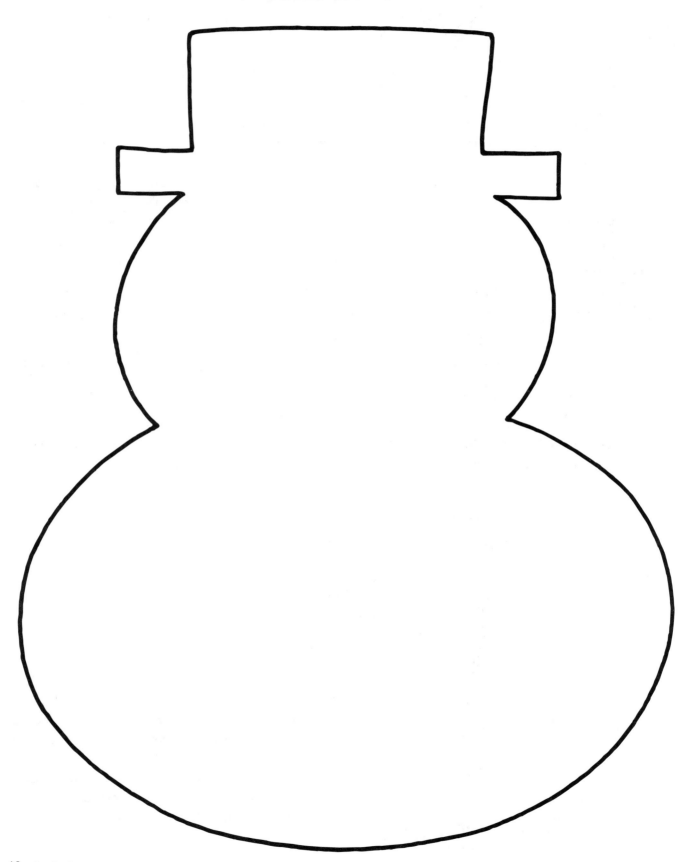

Bookmaking Bonanza © 2004 Creative Teaching Press

Materials

- ✓ white paper
- ✓ 9" x 12" (23 cm x 30.5 cm) construction paper (assorted colors)
- ✓ rubber bands
- ✓ straws
- ✓ hole punch
- ✓ long, firm objects (optional)

Rubber Band and Straw Books

Give each child several pieces of white paper, two pieces of construction paper, two rubber bands, and a straw. Invite children to place their white paper between the construction paper and hole-punch four holes along one side. Show them how to insert from the back of the book a rubber band through the top hole, hold the end, and insert from the back of the book the other end through the next hole. Tell children to insert one end of a straw through both ends and release the rubber band. Have children insert a rubber band through the third hole, hold the end, and insert the other end through the last hole. Ask children to insert the remaining part of the straw through both ends and release the rubber band. As an option, have children use a different long, firm object, such as a stick or a feather, to bind the book.

The Happy Birthday Book

by Room 2

Happy Birthday!

Skills
✓ identifying months of the year
✓ arranging in chronological order

Take a photograph of each child in class. Give each child a **Happy Birthday reproducible (page 65)** and his or her photo to glue on the paper. Tell children to write their name and the month in which they were born in the spaces provided. As an option, give children festive **stickers** to attach to their page. Invite children to help you arrange the pages in chronological order. Use the directions on page 63 to make a rubber band and straw class book. Write *The Happy Birthday Book* on the front cover. As an option, use two birthday candles instead of a straw. Place the book in the class library.

What Is in Your Lunch?

Skills
✓ spelling
✓ writing addition sentences

Give each child a piece of **white paper.** Have children place their paper in a landscape position and draw foods, glue foods cut out from **construction paper,** or glue empty, clean **food wrappers** to their page. Encourage children to write the name of their foods above their pictures. Have children write an addition sentence below their drawings, cutouts, or wrappers. Follow the directions on page 63 to make a rubber band and straw class book. Then, cut the cover into a lunchbox shape, and write *What Is in Your Lunch?* on it. Place the book in the class library.

I ate a sandwich and two cookies.

$1 + 2 = 3$

Happy Birthday

Happy Birthday to _____!

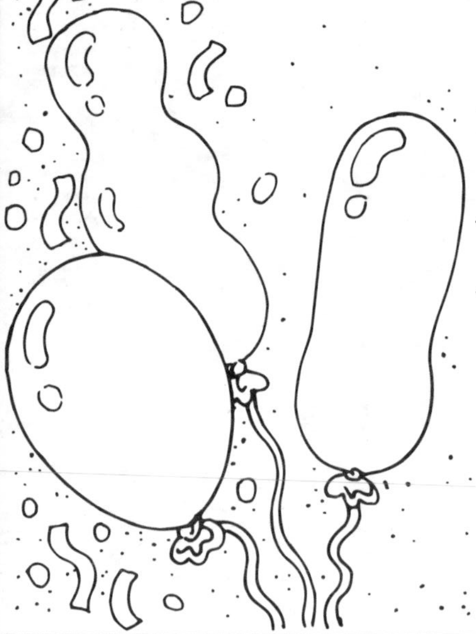

(month)

Necklace Books

Materials
✓ copy paper
✓ scissors
✓ yarn or string

Ask parent volunteers to help you use these directions to make a necklace book for each child. Fold a piece of paper in half lengthwise. Fold it again in the same direction, and then open it. Fold the paper in half widthwise, and open it again. Unfold the paper to reveal a set of two intersecting creased lines. Position scissors on the vertical creased line at the folded edge and cut to the intersection. Unfold the paper, and refold it widthwise. Push together the edges of the paper until the center of the book expands and four pages are created. Fold the pages into a book. Invite children to write a title and their name on the front cover and a story on the pages of their book. Insert a piece of yarn or string through the center of each book and tie together the ends to make a necklace book.

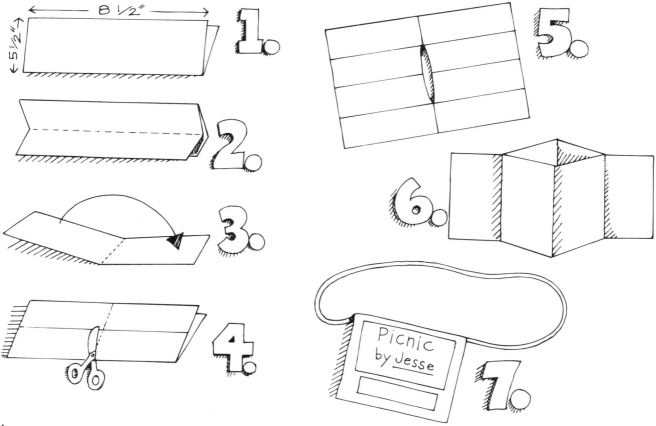

A Picnic for Your Senses

Skills

✓ exploring the five senses

✓ improving fluency

Ask children to name their five senses. Tell children they are going to write a book about how they use their senses at a picnic. Give each child a **necklace book (see page 66)** and a **Picnic reproducible (page 68)** to color and cut apart. Tell children to write their name after the title and then glue it to the cover of their book. Ask them to glue the pictures in order to separate pages of their book. Have children name the picture on the first page. Ask them to find the matching word card and glue it near the picture. Invite children to repeat the steps with the remaining four pages. As an option, give children a small piece of fabric to glue over the picnic blanket that coordinates with the phrase *I touch*.

My Book of -ing

Skills

✓ using suffixes

✓ improving fluency

Say *I can sleep*. Pantomime that you are sleeping, and say *I am sleeping*. Ask children to name things they can do. Invite a volunteer to complete the frame *I can _____*. Ask him or her to act out the activity. Say *You are _____*. Complete the frame with the action word. Emphasize for children that these action words end with *-ing*. Give each child a **necklace book (see page 66)** and a **My Book of -ing reproducible (page 69)** to color and cut apart. Tell children to write their name after the title and glue it to the cover of their book. Ask children to glue a picture card on each page of their book. Have them name the picture on the first page and write *-ing* on each blank line. Encourage children to read their new *-ing* word. Invite them to repeat these steps with the remaining four pages.

Picnic

The Picnic by _____	I smell 3
I hear 1	I taste 4
I touch 2	I see a picnic! 5

My Book of -ing

by _____

sleep _____   1

eat _____   2

talk _____   3

sing _____   4

read _____   5

Shape Books

✓ reproducible patterns (pages 73–74)
✓ tagboard
✓ scissors
✓ white copy paper
✓ 9" x 12" (23 cm x 30.5 cm) construction paper
✓ stapler
✓ art supplies (e.g., crayons, markers, glitter, ribbon, stickers)

Make your own pattern, or choose one of the reproducible patterns, copy it on tagboard, and cut it out. Repeat these steps to make several patterns for the class to share. Give each child several sheets of white copy paper and a piece of construction paper to place on top. Show children how to place the tagboard pattern on top of the papers and trace around it. Tell them to cut along the line and through all the papers. Have children staple together their papers to make a shape book. Invite them to use art supplies to decorate their cover.

What Does Bee See?
by Rob

Ladybug Spots

Skills

✓ writing number words
✓ counting
✓ improving fluency

Use the reproducible **ladybug pattern (page 73)** and the directions on page 70 to help children make a five-page shape book. Write *Ladybug Spots!* on the board, and tell children to write it and their name on the cover of their book. Give each child a pair of **wiggly eyes** to glue to the ladybug's face. Write on the board *I have ___ dots.* Ask children to copy the sentence frame on the bottom of each page of their book. Ask them to use a **black crayon or marker** to draw a set of less than ten dots on each page. Have children write the word for the number of dots on the line of each sentence frame. Invite children to read each other's books.

Stocking Stuffers

Skills

✓ writing sentences
✓ improving fluency

Use the reproducible **stocking pattern (page 73)** and the directions on page 70 to help children make a six-page shape book. Discuss with children the Christmas Eve tradition of hanging a stocking beside a fireplace or on a bedpost. Write *Wish List* at the top of a piece of **chart paper.** Invite children to name items they would like to receive. Encourage them to sound out the name of each item as you write the letters of the word. Ask children to write their name in the frame _____'s *Wishes* on the cover of their book. Give children **catalogs or flyers for toy stores,** and have them cut out pictures of items they would like. Tell children to glue one picture at the top of each remaining page of their book. Write on the board *I would like _____.* Have children copy the sentence frame on the bottom of each page. Ask them to complete each frame with the name of the object above it. Display the completed shape books on a bulletin board titled *Our Stockings Full of Wishes.*

What Does Bee See?

Use the reproducible **bee pattern (page 74)** and the directions on page 70 to help children make a five-page shape book. Tell children to add **black construction paper** antennae, stripes, and a stinger. Have children draw a face on their bee and write *What Does Bee See?* and their name on one of the wings. Write on the board *Bee sees a ____.* Have children write the frame on each page of their book. Invite them to think of words that begin with /b/ (e.g., *bear, baby, bug*) and write one word to complete the frame on each page. Encourage children to glue a picture cut out from a magazine, attach a sticker, or draw a picture to illustrate each sentence.

Ant Can't, But I Can!

Use the reproducible **ant pattern (page 74)** and the directions on page 70 to help children make a five-page shape book. Tell children to cut two antennae and six legs from **black construction paper** and glue them on their ant. Have children draw a face on their ant and write *Ant Can't, But I Can!* and their name on the front cover. Write on the board *Ant can't ____, but I can.* Have children write the frame on each page of their book. Invite them to think of things they can do that an ant can't (e.g., ride a bike or read a book) and write one idea to complete the frame on each page. Encourage children to glue a picture cut out from a magazine, attach a sticker, or draw a picture to illustrate each sentence.

Patterns

ladybug

stocking

Patterns

bee

ant

Bookmaking Bonanza © 2004 Creative Teaching Press

Die Cut Books

Materials

✓ die cut letters or shapes
✓ copy paper
✓ scissors
✓ stapler

Give each child a die cut letter or shape and some paper. Show children how to cut around their letter or shape and through the paper. Ask children to staple together their papers to make a book.

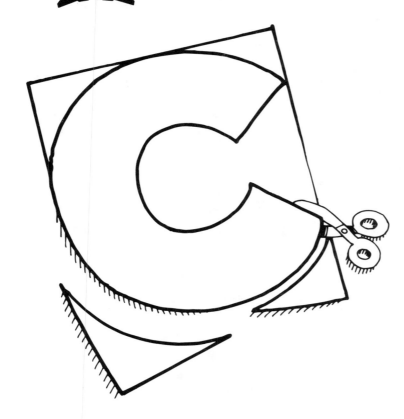

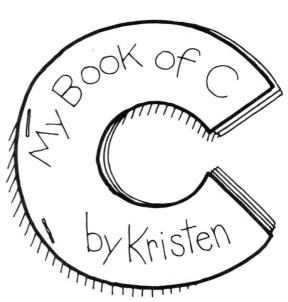

My Book of C by Kristen

Alphabet Books

Skills
✓ identifying letters
✓ counting

Choose a **die cut letter (e.g., A),** and give one to each child. Use the directions on page 75 to help children make a five-page book. Ask children to write a number from one to ten on each page of their book to indicate how many copies of the letter from the cover should appear on the page. Tell children to turn to the first page, identify the number (e.g., 3), cut from a **magazine or a newspaper** that many copies of their letter, and glue them to the page. Encourage children to repeat the steps on the remaining pages.

F Is for Fish

Skills
✓ identifying beginning sounds
✓ writing sentences

Choose a **die cut letter (e.g., F),** and give one to each child. Use the directions on page 75 to help children make a five-page book. Ask children to draw or glue on each page of their book a picture that begins with their letter. Encourage children to use the name of their letter and each object to complete the sentence frame ___ *is for* ____. Have children write it below each picture. Ask them to repeat the steps with the remaining pages.

Sh Is for Shell

Skill
✓ identifying blends and digraphs

Choose a **die cut shape (e.g., a shell),** and give one to each child. Use the directions on page 75 to help children make a five-page book. Invite children to name the object on their cover and its beginning sound. Ask them to name things that begin with the sound and draw or glue on each page of their book a picture that begins with it. Encourage children to use the name of their letter and each object to complete the sentence frame ___ *is for* ____. Have children write it below each picture. Ask them to repeat the steps with the remaining pages. Tell children to write the title *Sh Is for Shell* and their name on the cover of their book.

Photo Album Books

Materials

✓ photo albums
✓ photographs or magazine pictures
✓ index cards or paper

Collect inexpensive photo albums, and place photographs of class events or pictures cut from magazines on alternate pages. Invite children to write on index cards or pieces of paper captions for the images, and place them on the pages beside the corresponding pictures.

Down on the Farm Photo Album

Give individual children or pairs of children a piece of **paper** and a **photograph from a class field trip to a farm or a magazine picture of a farm.** Ask children to glue their picture on their paper and write a description below it. Place the pages in a **photo album.** Write *Down on the Farm* on the cover, and decorate it with **stickers of farm animals.** Invite children to take turns bringing the album home to share with their families.

Our Little Book of Numbers

Give individual children or pairs of children a piece of **paper** and assign them a number from one to five. Tell children to write the word for their number at the top of their paper. Ask them to glue the same number of **magazine pictures** or draw the same number of pictures on their paper. Encourage children to write a sentence to describe their pictures, such as *We have five toys.* Place the pages in a **photo album,** and write *Our Little Book of Numbers* on the cover.

Photocopied Picture Books

Photograph individual or small groups of children, and make several copies of the pictures to use as book covers. Have children place their photocopied picture on top of five pieces of paper, cut around it and through the papers, and staple them together. Or, invite children to use the photocopied pictures as illustrations in other books.

Materials

✓ camera
✓ film
✓ paper
✓ stapler

My Number 2 Book
by Sydney

M Is for Me!

Skills

✓ identifying beginning sounds
✓ writing sentences
✓ improving fluency

Photograph individual children, and copy the **pictures.** Give each child his or her own picture. Use the directions on page 79 to help children make a five-page book. Ask children to identify the first sound of their name. Tell them to use the letter and their name to complete the frame ___ *is for* _____! (e.g., *L is for Lois!*), and write it across their picture. Ask children to draw or glue on each page of their book a picture of something that begins with the first letter of their name (e.g., ladybug). Tell children to use their letter and words to complete the sentence frame (e.g., *L is for ladybugs*) and write it below each picture. When children have completed their books, invite those whose name begins with *A* to read aloud their books. Repeat with the remaining letters in alphabetical order.

How Many in All?

Skills

✓ counting
✓ writing sentences
✓ writing number sentences

Photograph a group of two, three, four, and five children; copy their **pictures;** and give each child a group picture he or she appears in. Use the directions on page 79 to help children make a five-page book. Give each child a **construction paper strip,** and ask children to write *My Number ___ Book* on it. Tell them to write the number of children in the picture on the blank line and glue their strip to their cover. Ask children to cut from **magazines** pictures that show two similar things (e.g., bicycles, apples) or two things in a set (e.g., feet, twin babies) and glue them to separate pages of their book. Invite children to write sentences that describe their pictures below them. Then, encourage children to write a number sentence (e.g., *2 + 0 = 2*) for each picture. Place the books in the class library.